IMAGES
of Sport

THIRD LANARK
ATHLETIC CLUB

The name never dies – Third Lanark in 1997, for a friendly match against Greenock North Over-50s. The ex-Thirds players are, from left to right: Evan Williams, Hugh McLaughlin, David Brady, Alan McKay, Tony Connell.

IMAGES
of Sport

THIRD LANARK
ATHLETIC CLUB

Compiled by
Bob Laird

TEMPUS

First published 1999
Copyright © Bob Laird, 1999

Tempus Publishing Limited
The Mill, Brimscombe Port,
Stroud, Gloucestershire, GL5 2QG

ISBN 0 7524 1850 5

Typesetting and origination by
Tempus Publishing Limited
Printed in Great Britain by
Midway Clark Printing, Wiltshire

The 1996/97 Player of the Year Awards, and the author receives an award for his dedication to Third Lanark.

Contents

The Third Lanrkshire Rifle Volunteers in 1872, the year the football team was founded.

Acknowledgements

The author would like to thank *The Herald* and *Evening Times*, and the *Daily Record* and *Sunday Mail*, for the reproduction of some of the photographs. Thanks also to Jack Murray for the use of two Third Lanark postcards.

Introduction

Third Lanark Athletic Club was borne from the Regiment of the Third Lanarkshire Rifle Volunteers in 1872 after the first Scotland *v.* England international. This inspired the regiment to start a football team, the club becoming one of the original members of the Scottish Football Association, and in 1890, an original member of the Scottish League. Throughout their history, the club was always based on the Southside of Glasgow. They moved into where Cathkin Park is today after purchasing the ground from Queens Park.

The club's most successful period was in the early 1900s when they won the First Division Championship for the only time in their history; they also won the Scottish Cup, Glasgow Cup, Charity Cup and the Inter City League in this period. Some famous names played for Thirds, such as Tod Sloan, who captained the team in the successful early 1900s, and goalkeeper Jimmy Brownlie. The 1930s brought Neilly Dewar, Jimmy Carabine and Jimmy Mason, while the fifties and sixties saw the era of star goalkeeper wee Jocky Robertson, and the forward line of Goodfellow, Hilley, Harley, Gray and McInnes, who in season 1960/61 scored 100 goals in 34 League games. Unfortunately, the defence lost 80 goals as the club finished third in the First Division.

Third Lanark became a limited company in 1903, dropped the regimental title from their name and registered as Third Lanark Athletic Club, playing in scarlet jerseys from then until their demise in 1967. They were affectionately known as the 'Hi Hi', and to this day there has never been a credible explanation for this. Early information states that the Cathkin whisper was 'Hi, Hi, Hi', and throughout the years I have heard a few different reasons for this. The Cathkin turf was reputed to be the best in Scotland, although it helped other teams as well!

When official football resumed after the Second World War, the club was in the First Division, but were relegated after the 1952/53 season. Promotion was won in 1956/57 and Thirds seemed to be going places when they went full-time in 1960 under manager George Young. Success in the 1960/61 season and a third place finish, however, attracted interest in their players, and Hilley, Harley and Gray were all transferred to English teams one after the other.

Third Lanark was then subject to a takeover in December 1962, and at the meeting a director who had previously been put off the board in the 1950s gained control of the club. Manager George Young resigned immediately, and from then on it was all downhill. A new stand was built but never finished, and attempts were made to move the club to the new town of East Kilbride so that Cathkin, which was in a prime site, could be sold off. This did not succeed and in the 1964/65 season Thirds were relegated with a total of 7 points – after 34 games they had won 3 and drawn 1. The support dwindled from a 35,000 crowd in the Scottish Cup Quarter-final against Hibernian in 1959 to 500 in 1967. The liquidators were called in as bills were left unpaid and opposition teams did not receive their share of the gate money. The end eventually came on Friday 28 April 1967 when the club played their last game at Dumbarton, losing 5-1 with Drew Busby scoring the last Thirds goal. They were gone.

On a brighter note, I have tried to include as many players who donned the Thirds jersey as I could, although some had to miss out for various reasons. This pictorial history, I am sure, will bring back a lot of memories, and in addition to photographs, I have included programme covers, ticket stubs and letters, to give a flavour of what the club was like.

One
In The Beginning

Third Lanark, 1888/89, Scottish Cup holders. From left to right, back row: A. Thompson, R. Downie, J. Rae. Middle row: J. Marshall, J. Thomson (Um), R. McFarlane, A. Lochead, W. French (Matchday Secretary), J. Hannah. Front row: John Oswald, W. Brown (President), W. Johnstone. Seated on ground: James Oswald, J. Auld.

HOW THIRD LANARK WAS BORN

Report of a Memorable Meeting

THIS, the first minute of the first meeting of what is to-day known as Third Lanark A.C. places in print the names of those enthusiasts who pioneered the club. Their names deserve an honoured place in the history of Third Lanark.

Seventy-five years ago a meeting of members of the Third Regiment of Lanarkshire Rifle Volunteers was held in the 3rd L.R.V. Orderly Room, East Howard Street. The date was December 12th, 1872, intimation having been given by public notice.

Private Broadfoot explained that the meeting was called for the purpose of organising, if possible, a Football Club in connection with the Third Regiment. He further reported that the Lieutenant-Colonel, the majority of the Officers, and twenty-five other members of the Regiment had signified their willingness to support such a club.

Sergeant Ralston then moved : " That we, the Members now assembled, should form ourselves into a club, to be called the 3rd L.R.V. Football Club." The motion was seconded by Private Taylor, and unanimously approved of.

Private McKinnon proposed that Lieut.-Col. H. E. Crum-Ewing be elected Honorary President. Col.-Sergt. Provan seconded this motion.

Private Broadfoot moved that Majors Robson and Forrester be elected Honorary Vice-Presidents. Private McDonald seconded this motion.

Private Broadfoot moved that Captain Inglis be elected President of the Club, Sergeant Ralston seconded the motion.

Sergeant Ralston moved that Ensign Masson be elected Vice-President of the Club. Private McKinnon seconded the motion.

Sergeant Ralston moved that private Broadfoot be elected Captain of the Club. Private McKinnon seconded the motion. Private McKinnon proposed that Sergeant Haswell be elected Treasurer for the Club. Col.-Sergt. Provan seconded the motion.

Private Broadfoot proposed that Private R. Moodie be elected Secretary. Sergt. Ralston seconded the motion.

The members then nominated a Committee of eight, namely :—Col.-Sergt. Provan, Sergt.

Ralston, Sergeant W. McOnie, Private Tom Stewart, Private MacKinnon, Private Jos. Taylor, Private Stewart, Private Jas. Donald.

Following constitution was then drawn up and adopted :—

RULE I.—That this Club be called the 3rd L.R.V. Football Club.

RULE II.—That the annual subscription be two shillings and sixpence per member, payable in advance.

RULE III.—That the office-bearers consist of One Honorary President, Two Honorary Vice-Presidents, a President, a Vice-President, a Treasurer, a Secretary, a Captain, and eight members of committee, five to form a quorum.

RULE IV.—That the office-bearers be elected at the Annual General Meeting, retiring office-bearers being eligible for re-election.

RULE V.—That Members of the Regiment only be admitted to the Club.

RULE VI.—That the Club play according to the Rules of the Football Association, and also that it join the Association.

RULE VII.—That the Annual General Meeting be held on the first Thursday of March.

RULE VIII.—That any alteration in the above laws or constitution of this Club can only be made at the Annual General Meeting ; and notice thereof must be given to the Secretary in writing on or before the fifteenth of February previous.

(Signed) JOHN INGLIS,
Chairman.

A report detailing the birth of Third Lanark.

The Third Lanark team which won the Charity Cup in the 1889/90 season

Third Lanark, 1897/98. From left to right, back row: Alex McNab (Secretary), James Simpson, Robert Barr (Captain), George McCue, Alex Milne, David Gardner, Alex Duncan (Trainer). Front row: James Gillespie, Herbert Banks, James Hannah, James Smith. Seated on ground: Robert Beveridge, Robert Johnson.

Third Lanark, 1898/99.

Glasgow International Exhibition, 1901.

>•<

Third Lanark Football Club.

Annual

Tournament

IN THE

EXHIBITION SPORTS GROUND,

ON

SATURDAY, 27th July, 1901,

Commencing at 3.30 p.m.

A programme of events as part of the Glasgow International Exhibition. Included were a five-a-side football tournament, a gymnastics display and a novelty potato race.

13

Above and below: Early action shots from Cathkin before Thirds moved up the hill to where the ground is at present. The photographs are from 1901/02 and the picture below features Hugh Wilson, who went on to play such an important part in the League and Cup success between 1903 and 1905.

Opposite: A 1902 Newcastle United programme for a friendly against Third Lanark Rifle Volunteers. This is a single sheet printed on both sides.

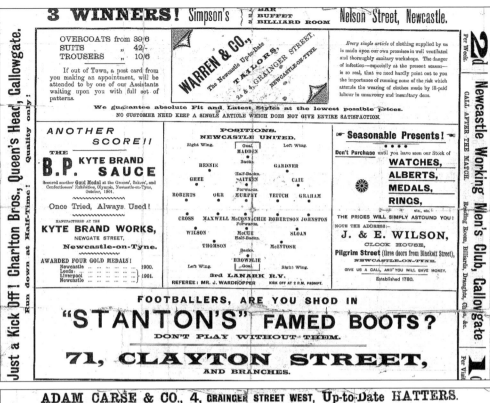

Third Lanark, 1903/04, Glasgow Cup holders. From left to right, back row: F. Haven (Manager and Secretary), R. Woodburn (Linesman), J. Neilson, T. Sloan, J. Cross, J. Raeside, J. Campbell, J. Campbell (Trainer). Front row: J. Johnston, R. Barr, R. Graham, H. Wilson (Captain), T. McKenzie, W. Wardrop, W. McIntosh.

Third Lanark, 1908/09. From left to right, back row: E.M. Tarbat (Secretary), T. Sloan, R. Ferguson, J. Brownlie, J.A. Dickson, J. Cross. R. Barr, J. Campbell (Trainer) Front row: T. Fairfoull, J. Kidd, J. McFie, A.M. Ballantine (President), D.A. Hill, W. McIntosh, J. Richardson. Seated on ground: J. Johnstone, R. Hosie.

16

Third Lanark, Scottish League Champions, 1903/04. From left to right, back row: Graham, Raeside, Sloan, Campbell, Neilson, Cross. Front row: Barr, McIntosh, McKenzie, J.B. Livingstone (Chairman), Wilson, Johnston, Wardrope.

Third Lanark, Scottish Cup Winners, 1904/05. From left to right, back row: J. Campbell (Trainer), Neilson, Campbell, Raeside, Sloan, Kelso, Comrie, S.M. Wylie (Secretary). Front row: McIntosh, McKenzie, Wilson, C. McDonald (Director), J.B. Livingstone (Chairman), Kidd, Barr. Seated on ground: Munro, Johnstone.

Jimmy Brownlie.

Jimmy Brownlie made his debut on 15 August 1906 against Partick Thistle, and his last game took place against St Mirren on 30 December 1922. In between, he became the most capped player in Thirds history, gaining sixteen full international caps. He also played in fourteen League internationals and in the Victory internationals of 1918/19.

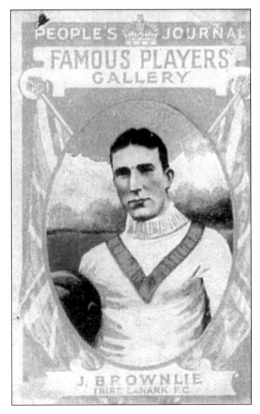

Without doubt, Jimmy was Thirds' longest serving goalkeeper, but maybe not the most successful. James Raeside has that distinction, playing in the successful early 1900s team. However, Jimmy was more famous and was once voted the most popular player in Scotland. He was even known to take a penalty, and did so against Motherwell on 9 September 1911, scoring in a 2-1 loss. Jimmy went on to manage Dundee United after his illustrious career with Thirds had finished.

Transferred from Sunderland, Hugh Wilson made his debut in the Charity Cup Final against Celtic on 9 May 1901. Thirds won the cup after a replay and Wilson scored. He played a big part in the League Championship of 1903/04 and the Scottish Cup win of 1904/05 when he scored twice as Thirds beat Rangers 3-1.

Robert Barr was a full-back throughout his career with Thirds who won League Championship, Charity, Glasgow and Scottish Cup medals in the early 1900s. Robert played his last game on 18 December 1909.

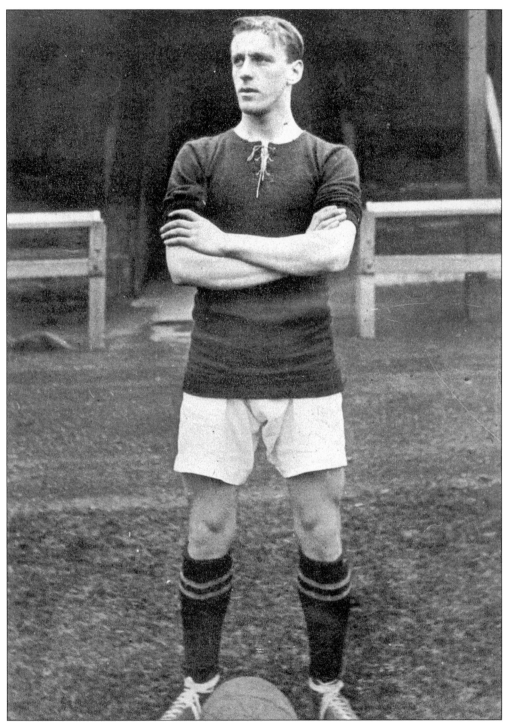

Bobby Orr made his debut on Christmas Day 1909 and played his last game on 21 April 1924. A loyal servant, he played full-back and was selected to play in four League internationals. Bobby also featured in the 1921 Scotland tour of Canada, sponsored by Thirds, and the tour of South America in 1923.

Above and opposite: Two early Third Lanark postcards.

THE
Third Lanark Athletic Club,
LIMITED

GROUND—
CATHKIN PARK, CATHCART ROAD,
CROSSHILL.

SEASON 1911-1912

ADMIT TO GROUND & STAND

W. *Thos. Foote*

Laura Cottage
Millerston

Edm. Tarbat

Secretary

AVAILABLE TILL 30th APRIL, 1912

Left and below: Two season tickets from 1911/12 and 1919/20. The latter was a shareholder's season ticket.

THE 68
Third Lanark Athletic Club
Limited

GROUND—
CATHKIN PARK, CATHCART ROAD,
CROSSHILL.

SEASON 1919-1920

ADMIT TO GROUND & STAND

Thos Foote

Laura Cottage
Millerston

Geo Morrell
Secy.

Shareholder's Ticket, 5/-
Tax, 5/9 /9

Available till 30th APRIL, 1920.

Two
The Twenties And Thirties

A Third Lanark shield.

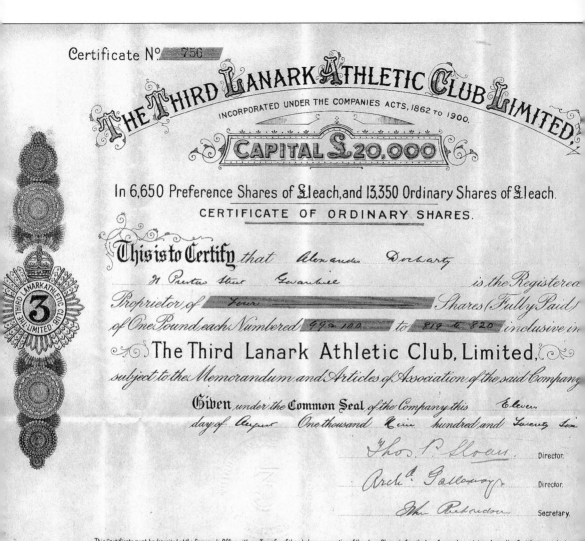

Certificate Nº 756

The Third Lanark Athletic Club Limited,

INCORPORATED UNDER THE COMPANIES ACTS, 1862 TO 1900.

CAPITAL £20,000

In 6,650 Preference Shares of £1 each, and 13,350 Ordinary Shares of £1 each.

CERTIFICATE OF ORDINARY SHARES.

This is to Certify that *Alexander Doherty*

71 Preston Street Govanhill is the Registered Proprietor of *Four* Shares (Fully Paid) of One Pound each. Numbered *997 120* to *819 & 820* inclusive in

The Third Lanark Athletic Club, Limited,

subject to the Memorandum and Articles of Association of the said Company

Given under the Common Seal of the Company this *Eleven* day of *August* One thousand Nine hundred and *Twenty Six*

Thos. P. Sloan — Director.

Archd. Galloway — Director.

John Richardson — Secretary.

This Certificate must be deposited at the Company's Office with any Transfer of the whole or any portion of the above Shares before the transfer can be registered or a New Certificate can be issued

REGISTERED OFFICE OF THE COMPANY, CATHKIN PARK.

A beautifully presented share certificate from 1926. The quality of the paper was excellent and it was printed in both blue and red headings.

Third Lanark, 1921/22. From left to right, back row: Slavin, I. Walker, Brownlie, Wilson, Findlay. Front row: Anderson, Reid, Orr, J. Walker, Allan, F. Walker.

Third Lanark, 1922/23. From left to right, back row: Knox, Findlay, Orr, Brownlie, McKenna, Gilchrist. Front row: Walker, Reid, McCormack, Paton, F. Walker.

Jimmy Denmark made his debut on 16 September 1931 in a 6-0 defeat by Motherwell, going on to establish himself as centre half in the Thirds team and captaining the club against Rangers in the 1935/36 Scottish Cup Final. He played his last match on 1 May 1937 and was transferred to Newcastle United.

Robert Kennedy made his debut on 11 August 1934. An inside forward, he won a B Division championship medal and played his part in the Scottish Cup run and final in 1936, where Rangers beat Thirds 1-0. He played his last match on 12 November 1938.

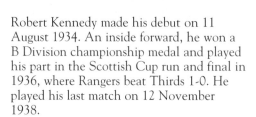

A rare Third Lanark postcard from the 1921/22 season. From left to right, back row: Walker, Biggar (Assistant Trainer), McAndrew, Scott, Slavin, Brownlie, Findley, J. Walker, W. Biggar (Trainer). Front row: Reid, F. Walker, Orr, Anderson, Hillhouse.

Third Lanark, 1924/25. From left to right, back row: Finlay, Brown, Jarvie, Frame, Williamson. Front row: McInally, Reid, J. Walker, F. Walker, Archibald.

A truly loyal servant to the club, Sam Brown was a full-back who made his debut on 25 September 1922 and played his last game on 20 October 1928. He joined the backroom staff at Cathkin and was still connected to the club in 1960.

John Lynas made his debut on 5 October 1929 against Armadale. He was an outside right and featured in the forward line of Lynas, Jack, Dewar, Blair and Breslin. He won Second Division championship medals in 1930/31 and 1934/35, playing his last game against Rangers on 4 May 1935.

Third Lanark, 1928/29. From left to right, back row: Stevenson, Jamieson, Allan, Mill, Mitchell, Muir. Front row: Calligan, Halliday, Wilson, Hamill, Thomson.

Third Lanark, Second Division Champions, 1930/31. From left to right, back row: Moreland, G. Clark, Simpson, Waugh, Warden, McLellan. Front row: Lynas, Jack, Dewar Blair, Breslin.

Neilly Dewar made his debut on
2 November 1929 and scored twice
in a 4-2 win over Alloa Athletic. He
was transferred to Manchester United
in 1933 and went on to play for
Sheffield Wednesday before returning
to Thirds in 1937.

A prolific goalscorer, Neilly was the leading
goalscorer in every season that he played for
Third Lanark. He was capped three times
and scored a hat-trick in 1932 for Scotland
against France in Paris.

Third Lanark, 1929/1930. From left to right, back row: Moreland, MacPherson, Clarke, Waugh, Latter, McLelland. Front row: Lynas, Jack, Mitchell, Wallace, Perry.

Third Lanark, 1934/35. From left to right, back row: Blair, Denmark, McInnes, McCormack, Carabine, Harvey. Front row: Kinnaird, Gallagher, Hay, Kennedy, Howe.

The 1936 Scottish Cup Final, Rangers 1 Third Lanark 0. This was the club's last appearance in the Scottish Cup Final. Thirds' goalkeeper Muir and defenders Hamilton and Carabine are relieved to see the ball going over the bar.

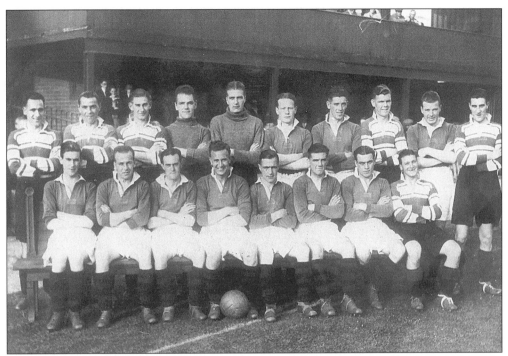

Third Lanark, 1935/36. From left to right, back row: Kennedy, Dobbs, Simpson, Muir, McCormack, Stewart, Gallagher, Lambie, Hamilton, Black. Front row: Harvey, Blair, Ritchie, Denmark, Howe, Carabine, Hay, Morrison.

Third Lanark, 1936/37. From left to right, back row: J. Wright, A. Hart, J. Craig, J. Mason, M. Morrison, J. McInnes, J. Harvey, W. Hutchison (Groundsman), R. Archibald (Assistant Trainer). Middle row: J. Black, H. Sharpe, J. Hall, R. Hamilton, R. Muir, J. Blair, A. Kinnaird, G. Hay, S. Brown (Assistant Trainer). Front row: J. Nelson (Trainer), R. Howe, P. Gallacher, J. Carabine, J. Denmark, A. Rhodie, R. Kennedy, A. Milne, D. Smith (Assistant Trainer).

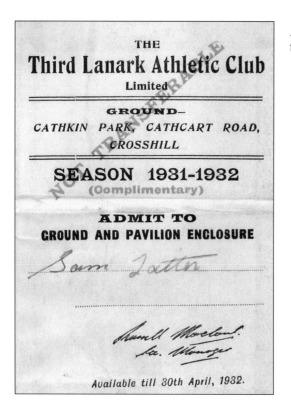

A 1931/32 player's ticket belonging to full-back Sam Latter.

Authographs from the 1937/38 season.

Three
The Forties

Third Lanark, 1946/47. From left to right, back row: Bolt, Balunas, Petrie, Kelly, Palmer, Mooney. Front row: Hart, Mason, Carabine, Venters, Mitchell.

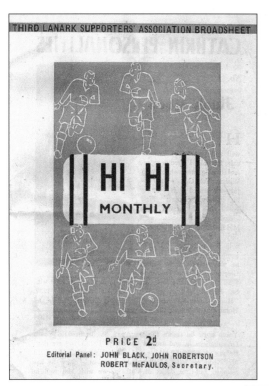

Hi Hi Monthly. This was the first publication after the war. The newly founded Supporters Association went ahead on their own to produce this item.

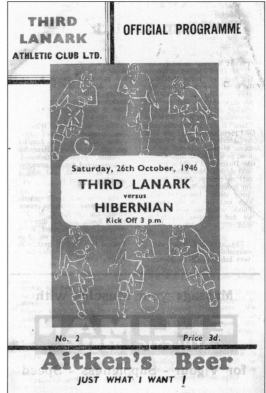

The club then agreed to a programme publication and the first programme was published against Celtic on 19 October 1946. Featured here is the second issue for the match against Hibs.

A change of format for programme number 6 in 1946.

Another change for the 1947/48 season.

Matt Balunas
Third Lanark F.C.

Matt Balunas and Johnny Kelly formed a great full-back partnership in the 1940s. Matt played on the right and Johnny played on the left. The team never looked the same if either of them were not playing.

Johnny Kelly

Johnny moved on in 1950 and Matt in 1955.

10 January 1948, League match at Cathkin, Third Lanark 4 Hearts 1. Flavell of Hearts shoots for goal as Mooney of Thirds tries to block the shot. They are watched by Currie of Hearts and Barclay of Thirds.

Third Lanark, 1946/47. From left to right, back row: Balunas, Kelly, Fraser, Bolt, Palmer, Mooney. Front row: Bogan, McDonald, McCulloch, Ayton, Mitchell.

Ian Proudfoot was a wing half who played for Thirds during the Second World War.

Adam McCulloch was a strong bustling type of centre forward who played for Thirds in the 1940s.

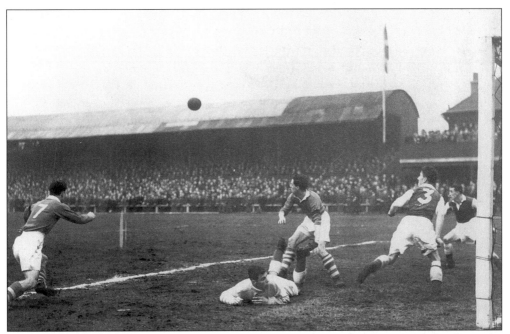

28 February 1948, League match at Cathkin, Third Lanark 1 Hibernian 4. An attack on the Hibs goal by Thirds wingers Staroscik and Mitchell. Goalkeeper Farm and full-backs Govan and Shaw are the Hibs defenders.

4 September 1948, League Match at Ibrox, Rangers 2 Third Lanark 1. Thirds goalkeeper Petrie saves from Williamson of Rangers, with Thirds defenders Barclay and Balunas in attendance.

Third Lanark, 1946/47. From left to right, back row: Henderson, Kelly, Petrie, Mitchell, Palmer, Mooney. Front row: B. Logan, Balunas, Middleton, Bolt, McCulloch, Ayton, H. Good.

Third Lanark, 1946/47. From left to right, back row: Ayres, Lang, Barclay, Fraser, Cameron, Hart. Front row: H. Good, Bogan, Baillie, Bryan, McDonald, Letters, B. Logan.

Third Lanark cartoon featuring Jimmy Harrower.

Third Lanark, 1948/49. From left to right, back row: Balunas, Orr, Fraser, Barclay, Mooney, Harrower. Front row: Henderson, Mason, Telford, Staroscik, Mitchell.

Bobby Mitchell was a goalscoring left winger who joined the club in the 1943/44 season. He played his last game on 5 February 1949 and was transferred to Newcastle United, where he had a very successful career

John Petrie was a stylish goalkeeper who vied for the goalkeeping position with Willie Fraser through the late 1940s. He suffered a broken leg in 1949 in a match against Stirling Albion.

2 May 1949, Charity Cup Semi-final at Hampden, Third Lanark 0 Celtic 2. Thirds goalkeeper Willie Fraser makes a great effort to save a penalty kick from Paton of Celtic.

3 May 1950, Charity Cup-tie at Hampden, Third Lanark 0 Celtic 1. Thirds goalkeeper Lewis Goram collects a high cross with full-back Matt Balunas on the goal line.

Jimmy Carabine.

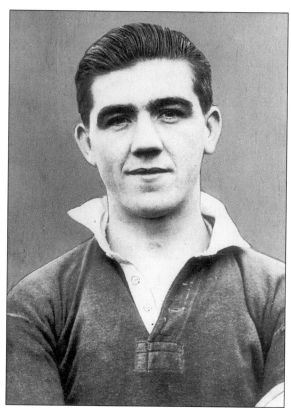

Jimmy Carabine was a full-back of tremendous skill who made his debut on 14 November 1931 against St Mirren. He played in the two full-back positions, centre half, outside right and centre forward – a truly versatile player! Jimmy won three international caps but was denied more due to the Second World War. He also played five times for the Scottish League and six times for Scotland during the war years, playing his last game for Thirds on 1 January 1947 against Queens Park. Jimmy went on to become manager of the team and was a great ambassador for the club.

A Jimmy Carabine cigarette card of the day.

The first design of the newly formed Supporters Association Card.

The
Third Lanark Athletic Club
Limited

GROUND :
CATHKIN PARK, CATHCART ROAD,
CROSSHILL.

NOT TRANSFERABLE.

LIFE MEMBER :

....

....

Admit to Ground and Stand.

ALEX. RITCHIE,
Secy.-Manager

A life membership ticket for the club.
Sadly, the club went first.

Left and below: Changes again in the programme format. This showed that three different formats were used in the 1947/48 season (see p.39).

Jimmy Mason.

Jimmy Mason or 'The Maestro' as he was affectionately known, due to his tremendous skill, was a real tanner ba' inside forward who played his first game on 8 August 1936 against Kilmarnock at Cathkin. He remained at the club until injury finished his career, playing his last game on 18 October 1952 against Motherwell.

Jimmy was capped seven times for Scotland and seven times for the Scottish League. His most notable international was against England at Wembley in 1949, when he notched the first goal in a 3-1 win. He received a testimonial from the club and the programme cover is featured later on p.82.

The Third Lanark programme *v.* Hibs on 19 April 1949.

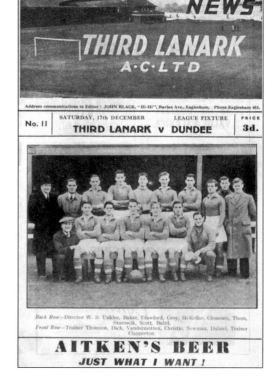

The Third Lanark programme *v.* Dundee on 17 December 1949. Yet again there have been more changes to the programme format!

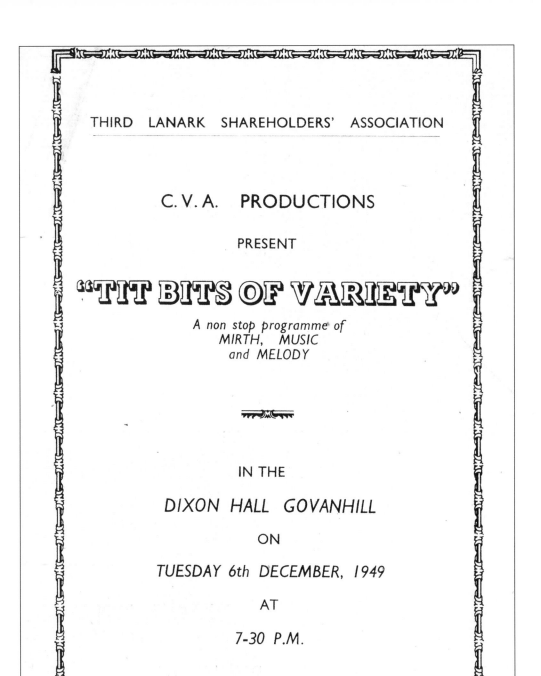

THIRD LANARK SHAREHOLDERS' ASSOCIATION

C. V. A. PRODUCTIONS

PRESENT

"TIT BITS OF VARIETY"

A non stop programme of
MIRTH, MUSIC
and MELODY

IN THE

DIXON HALL GOVANHILL

ON

TUESDAY 6th DECEMBER, 1949

AT

7-30 P.M.

Chairman - - - - - - - - - Mr. A. Caldwell

A concert to raise funds. There were seven different Artistes on the bill, ranging from Comedy, to Soprano, Hill Billy, Conjurer and Xylophone.

Ally McLeod was an outside left who made his debut on 5 November 1949, replacing Bobby Mitchell who had been transferred to Newcastle. He left the club in 1955/56, but returned again for one more season in 1963/64. Ally went into football management and eventually became manager of the Scottish national team.

George Aitken was a left half who was only at Thirds for a short spell. He made his debut on 10 February 1951 and played his last match on 17 November 1951, before being transferred to Sunderland.

Four

The Early Fifties

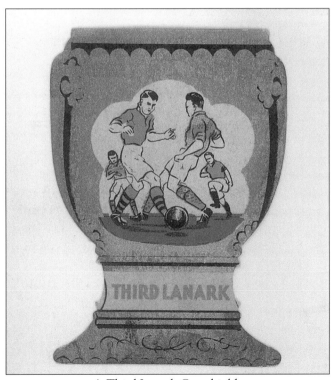

A Third Lanark Cup shield.

25 April 1951, League match at Cathkin, Third Lanark 1 Rangers 5. The horseshoe clearly did not bring much luck as Thirds defender Jimmy Harrower tries to stop the first of Rangers' five goals.

Jimmy Mason of Thirds is stretchered off in the same match after a collision with Ian McColl of Rangers.

Third Lanark line-up *v.* Celtic, 1950/51. From left to right, back row: Balunas, Harrower, Simpson, Orr, Christie, Mooney. Front row: Henderson, Mason, Muir, Cuthbertson, Staroscik.

Third Lanark line-up *v.* Raith Rovers, 1950/51. From left to right, back row: Balunas, Orr, Christie, Simpson, Harrower, Mooney. Front row: Henderson, Mason, Cuthbertson, Dick, Staroscik.

28 April 1951, League match at Cathkin, Third Lanark 2 Aberdeen 0. Goodall of Thirds heads for goal, watched by Harris and Young of Aberdeen and Henderson of Thirds

Action in the Aberdeen goalmouth. From left to right: Dick (Thirds), Lowrie, Martin and Young (all Aberdeen) and Goodall (Thirds).

Third Lanark, 1951/52. From left to right, back row: Heron, Cairns, Samuel, Forsyth, Whyte, Harrower, Balunas, Simpson. Middle row: Longridge, Smillie, Liddell, Dobbie, Robertson, Mason, McLeod. Front row: Goodall, Mooney, Phillips, Clements, Dick, Docherty.

Third Lanark, 1952/53. From left to right, back row: Balunas, Forsyth, Robertson, Mooney, Samuel, Duncan. Front row: Dobbie, Henderson, Cuthbertson, Dick, McLeod.

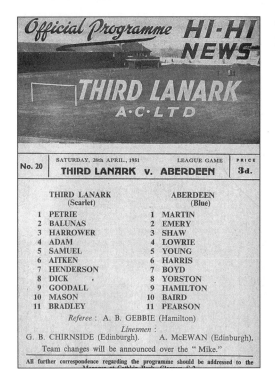

Third Lanark programme *v.* Aberdeen, 28 April 1951.

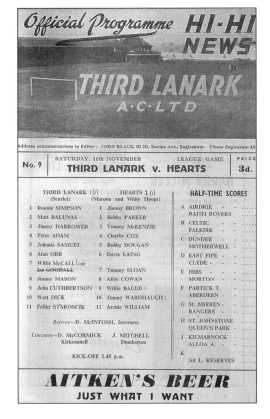

Third Lanark programme *v.* Hearts, 11 November 1951.

13 September, 1952. A League Cup-tie at Cathkin, Third Lanark 0 Rangers 0. Thirds 'keeper Robertson collects a cross whilst being challenged by Rangers' Willie Thornton.

20 October 1951, League match at Cathkin, Third Lanark 2 Aberdeen 0. Smellie of Thirds (on his debut) is challenged by Shaw of Aberdeen. The midweek afternoon kick-off clearly had an effect on the crowd!

8 November 1952, League match at Parkhead, Celtic 5 Third Lanark 4. Centre forward Cuthbertson of Thirds scores the first equalizer in a nine-goal thriller.

10 November, 1951, League Match at Cathkin, Third Lanark 1 East Fife 3. Thirds goalkeeper Petrie is well beaten.

12 January 1952, League match at Cathkin, Third Lanark 2 Queen of the South 1. Queens goalkeeper Henderson is beaten by a shot from Cuthbertson of Thirds for the winning goal.

24 November 1951, League match at Cathkin, Third Lanark 0 Motherwell 1. Thirds winger Ally McLeod scoops the ball over goalkeeper Johnstone but also over the bar. Onlookers are Henderson of Thirds, and Kilmarnock and McLeod of Motherwell.

15 January 1952, League Match at Love Street, St Mirren 3 Third Lanark 0. McGill of St Mirren is foiled by Thirds 'keeper Robertson, watched by defenders Forsyth and Balunas.

29 December 1951, League Match at Cathkin, Third Lanark 0 Dundee 2. Goalkeeper Henderson of Dundee dives at the feet of Thirds' Ally McLeod with defender Merchant in attendance.

1 January 1952, League match at Firhill, Partick Thistle 4 Third Lanark 2. Thirds golkeeper Jocky Robertson saves from Alex Stott of Partick Thistle.

THIRD LANARK A.C.
SUPPORTERS' ASSOCIATION

MEMBERSHIP
CARD

SEASON
1950-51

Founded - - February, 1946

Left and below: Two different styles of membership cards

MEMBERSHIP
CARD

SEASON
1954-55

FOUNDED — — FEBRUARY 1946

Jimmy Harrower leads out Jocky Robertson at Ibrox on 8 February 1954. This was a neutral venue for a third match against Stenhousemuir in the Scottish Cup as the teams had already drawn 2-2 and 0-0. Jimmy played at left-back and left half throughout his ten year service to the club.

30 January 1952, Scottish Cup tie at Parkhead, Celtic 0 Third Lanark 0. John McPhail and Bobby Collins of Celtic rush in as 'keeper Jocky Robertson saves, watched by defender Jimmy Cairns.

4 February 1952, Scottish Cup replay at Cathkin, Third Lanark 2 Celtic 1. Jimmy Docherty of Thirds scores the winning goal in extra time as he shoots past Celtic 'keeper Bonnar. Defenders Peacock and Stein look on.

29 March 1952, Scottish Cup Semi-final at Easter Road, Dundee 2 Third Lanark 0. Full-back Cairns of Thirds clears off the line with team-mates Robertson, Mooney and Balunas in attendance.

Burrell of Dundee puts the ball past Thirds 'keeper Robertson for the first goal in the 1952 Cup Semi-final. Defenders Cairns and Forsyth can only look on.

11 August 1951, League match at Parkhead, Celtic 1 Third Lanark 1. Celtic attack the Thirds goal. From left to right: Harrower, Mooney, Aitken, McCall(all Thirds), Fallon (Celtic), Petrie and Samuels (Thirds), and Peacock (Celtic).

14 April 1952, League match at Cathkin, Third Lanark 4 Hearts 0. Dick of Third Lanark fires past goalkeeper Brown and defender Adie to put Thirds one up.

7 May 1952, Charity Cup Semi-final at Ibrox, Rangers 0 Third Lanark 1. Rangers full-back George Young fails to intercept a cross and Third Lanark winger Ally McLeod heads home the only goal of the game.

8 August 1953, Third Lanark line-up for the opening League Cup-tie at Alloa. This was Thirds' first game in 'B' Division after being relegated and they beat Alloa 10-0.

10 May 1952. Charity Cup Final at Hampden, Third Lanark 2 Clyde 2. Goalkeeper Thomson of Clyde saves from Dobbie of Thirds. The cup was shared with each club keeping it for six months.

Third Lanark goalkeeper Robertson tips a shot over the bar as team-mates Forsyth and Mooney, and McPhail of Clyde, look on.

30 August 1952, League match at Cathkin, Third Lanark 2 East Fife 0. Charlie 'Legs' Fleming shoots for goal, watched by Thirds defender Jimmy Harrower.

6 September 1952, League match at Cathkin, Third Lanark 2 Hearts 3. McKenzie of Hearts makes a valiant attempt to stop Dick of Thirds from scoring, watched by Glidden and Parker of Hearts and Mason of Thirds.

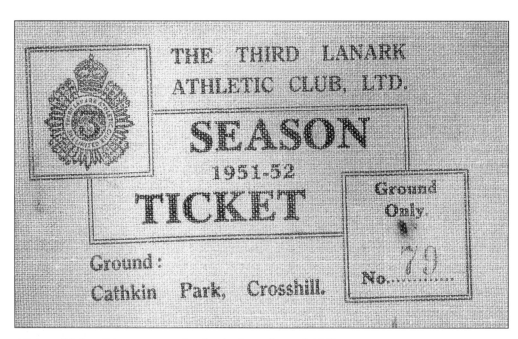

Above and below: Two season ticket books from the mid-1950s

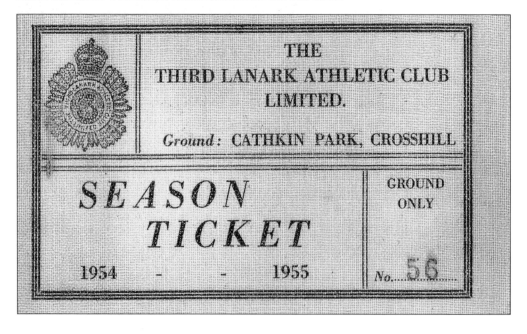

13 September 1952, League Cup-tie at Ibrox, Rangers 0 Third Lanark 0. Balunas of Thirds clears off the line as goalkeeper Robertson tries to save. Grierson of Rangers looks on.

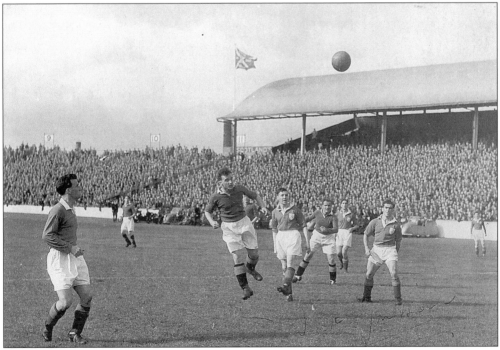

27 September 1952, League match at Ibrox, Rangers 4 Third Lanark 1. Grierson heads Rangers second goal, watched by Thirds defenders Harrower, Kennedy, Duncan and Mooney, and Thornton of Rangers.

22 November 1952, League match at Cathkin, Third Lanark 0 Dundee 0. Thirds centre forward Dobbie is on his own against three Dundee defenders.

12 April 1952, League match at Cathkin, Third Lanark 3 Celtic 3. Collins of Celtic scores. From left to right: Harrower (Thirds), Tully (Celtic), Robertson and Balunas (Thirds), Walsh (Celtic) and Mooney (Thirds).

Third Lanark in training for the start of the 1952/53 season. From left to right: Heron, Robertson, Docherty, Mooney, Mason, Henderson, Balunas, Simpson and Cairns.

1 November 1952 and Jimmy Mason talks to team-mates Harrower, McLeod, Samuels, Dick and Dobbie in the Cathkin dressing room. He had been told a few days earlier that he may never play again.

Third Lanark, 1954/55. From left to right, back row: Balunas, Harrower, Robertson, Kennedy, Philips. Front row: Barclay, Muir, Forsyth, Kerr, Dick, McLeod.

Third Lanark, 1955/56. From left to right, back row: Philips, Gordon, Petrie, Kennedy, Duncan, Jamieson, Rea, Miller, Dobbie, Gallagher, McLeod.

—FOUR CROWN—

CONVOY   All first class   **CAPE CLUB**
SHERRY   South African wines   **SHERRY**

sole proprietors

BULLOCH & CO., LIMITED

FROM LICENSED GROCERS & WINE MERCHANTS

14/6 per bottle & **7/9** per ½ bottle

THIRD LANARK A.C. LTD.

Official Programme

| No. 3 | SCOTTISH LEAGUE—'B' Division. SATURDAY, 22nd SEPT. THIRD LANARK v. CLYDE | Price 3d. |

AITKEN'S
EXPORT & STOUT
Just what I want!

In 1956 the programme format changed for the last time. This style of programme lasted until 1965. Interestingly, the price never changed from 3d from when the first programme was printed in 1946.

JAMES MASON
TESTIMONIAL GAME

SCOTLAND
SELECT

V.

SUNDERLAND

At

CATHKIN PARK

On

30th APRIL, 1953

Souvenir Programme
ONE SHILLING

The testimonial programme for Jimmy Mason, who had to retire from the game due to injury. He was at Cathkin from 1936 until 1952.

Five
The Late Fifties

Third Lanark, 1956/57. From left to right, back row: Smith, Gordon, Robertson, Kennedy, Maybury. Front row: Dobbie, Craig, Redpath, Wark, Roy, McInnes.

12 October 1957, League match at Cathkin, Third Lanark 0 Hearts 0. Thirds 'keeper Robertson saves from Bauld of Hearts with defenders Lewis and Cosker in attendance.

Here, Thirds 'keeper Robertson prevents Wardhaugh of Hearts from scoring, aided by centre half Lewis.

84

Third Lanark, 1956/57. From left to right, back row: Lewis, Kennedy, Robertson, Miller, Armstrong. Front row: Workman, Craig, Wark, Redpath, Roy, McInnes.

Third Lanark, 1956/57. From left to right, back row: Smith, Kennedy, Robertson, Lewis, Kelly, Brown. Front row: McInnes, McGuffie, Allan, Roy, Walker.

A Transport Section Membership Card. You paid 3/- (15p) per week home or away, and this covered the cost of away travel to support the team throughout the season.

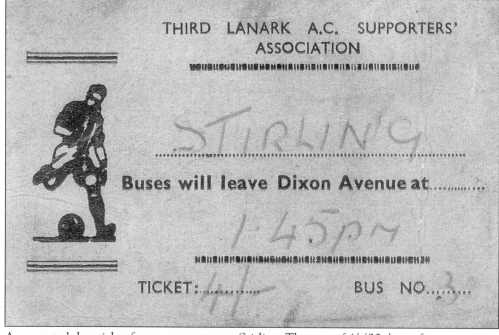

A supporter's bus ticket for an away game at Stirling. The cost of 4/-(20p) was for non-section transport members.

Jock Brown made his debut on 19 November 1955 against Forfar Athletic. He was a hard-tackling left-back who enjoyed using his shooting power at free-kicks. Jock played in the 1959 League Cup Final against Hearts and his last game was against Partick Thistle on 9 May 1960.

Johnny Allan was a centre forward who made his debut against Stranraer on 17 November 1956. His last game was on the 13 December 1958 against Falkirk. In the two full seasons Johnny played at Cathkin, he finished leading goalscorer with 30 and 39 goals respectively.

12 October 1957, League match at Cathkin. Third Lanark 0 Hearts 0. Thirds 'keeper Robertson saves a shot, watched by defenders Lewis and Brown.

26 October 1957, League match at Cathkin, Third Lanark 0 Celtic 2. Thirds 'keeper Robertson punches clear from McPhail of Celtic with defender Lewis in attendance.

A group of Third Lanark autographs from the 1957/58 season.

Tommy Docherty playing in a Thirds jersey against Partick Thistle in the 1956 Charity Cup Final. Thirds drafted in guest players to boost the gate. Ivor Broadis and ex-player Bobby Mitchell also played and Third Lanark won 4-2.

An unusual angle for a team photograph. This was the 1956/57 squad that won promotion, finishing runners-up to Clyde. Both teams had a high scoring season, with Clyde scoring 122 goals and Thirds scoring 105 goals in 36 League games.

Bob Shankly and Tom McNiven, manager and trainer in the late 1950s. The successful partnership was broken by Bob moving on to Dundee and Tom to Hibernian.

Third Lanark, 1957/58. From left to right, back row: Smith, Brown, Robertson, Slingsby, Lewis, Kelly. Front row: Carmichael, Cunningham, Catterson, Newman, Townsend.

Third Lanark, 1957/58. From left to right, back row: Stewart, Savage, Herd, McCrae, Cosker, Callaghan. Front row: W. Craig, R. Craig, Allan, Harley, McInnes.

GRAND OPENING FLOODLIGHT MATCH

THIRD LANARK

versus

BLACKPOOL

CATHKIN PARK

MONDAY, 30th NOVEMBER, 1959

The programme from Third Lanark *v.* Blackpool, the match that celebrated the opening of Cathkin's first set of floodlights.

The game ended in a 3-2 victory for Thirds. Referee Willie Brittle watches Jimmy Mason kicking off with Thirds players Goodfellow, Gray and Rankin in attendance.

GRAND OPENING

Floodlight Fixture

Third Lanark v. Blackpool

On MONDAY, 30th NOVEMBER, 1959

at

CATHKIN PARK . KICK-OFF 7.30 p.m.

Admit to—

EAST SECTION OF STAND

Price 6/-

A   10

A ticket for the East Section of the Stand.

The League Cup Final against Hearts in the 1959/60 season. Thirds opened the scoring after two minutes when Hearts 'keeper Marshall failed to collect a high ball and Matt Gray prodded the ball home. Hearts eventually won the match 2-1.

A great picture of Jocky Robertson in action with the cameras present. Jocky made his debut for Third Lanark on 22 December 1951 against Airdrie, and went on to play over 400 games for the club, his last against Dundee on 13 May 1963. At 5ft 5½in high, he was regarded as the smallest goalkeeper in Scotland, but his agility was second to none and he became a hero at Cathkin.

Third Lanark, 1959/60. From left to right: Moles, Smith, Robertson, Reilly, Cunningham, Caldwell. Front row: Hilley, Goodfellow, Rankine, Gray, McInnes.

Third Lanark, 1959/60. From left right, back row: Reilly, Cunningham, Caldwell. Font row: Gray, McInnes.

Six
Up, Down And Gone

Third Lanark, 1960/61 (100 goals scored and 80 lost). From left to right, back row: McGillivray, Caldwell, Robertson, Reilly, Robb, Cunningham. Front row: Goodfellow, Hilley, Harley, Gray, McInnes.

19 March 1960, League match at Cathkin, Third Lanark 2 Aberdeen 1. Matt Gray of Thirds opens the scoring by beating Aberdeen 'keeper Harkins and centre half Clunie.

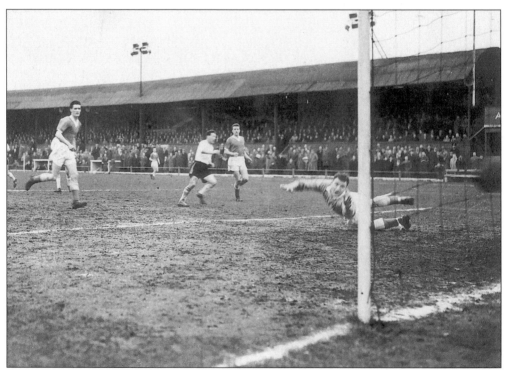

Thirds winger McInnes turns away after shooting past Harkins for the winning goal.

Third Lanark, 1960/61. From left to right, back row: Harley, Goodfellow, Gallagher, Brimms, Robertson, Reilly, Horne, McGillivray. Middle row: Cunningham, Denham, McCormack, Bowie, Ramage, McCallum, Caldwell, Brown, Gray. Front row: G. Young (Manager), McCool, Hilley, McBain, Lewis, Kerr, McInnes, Howley, T. McNiven (Trainer).

Third Lanark, 1961/62. From left to right, back row: McGillivray, Cunningham, McCormack, McLeod, Robertson, McKinlay, McCallum, Lewis, Gray, McCool. Front row: G. Young (Manager), Hilley, Harley, Reilly, W. McLean (Chairman), Goodfellow, McInally, McInnes, T. McNiven (Trainer).

Hilley, Harley and Gray on holiday in Spain.

The team that was fined by the SFA for playing a friendly match whilst on holiday in Spain. This was 1960 and the match was against local side Lloret del Mar. The Scottish Football Association were unhappy about the line-up for the friendly which included brothers Ian and Dave Hilley, Gray and Harley. Other big names in the line-up were Billy McNeill and Mike Jackson of Celtic and Jim McFadzean of Kilmarnock.

Matt Gray in trouble as he heads towards the SFA offices at Park Gardens.

12 August 1961. Thirds captain Jim Reilly leads out the team against Rangers, watched by team-mates Hilley and Harley. Both had refused to re-sign and missed the first game.

This League Cup-tie against Rangers was the opening match of the season at Cathkin in the 1961/62 season. The gates were closed before the kick-off but were then broken down by fans waiting to see the game. The terraces could not cope and the pitch was invaded. The players were taken off until order was restored by the police. The match was resumed with Rangers winning 2-0.

Dave Hilley made his debut at outside right against Hearts on 27 August 1958. He scored on his debut, but in a great match Hearts won 5-4. Dave moved to inside right and featured in the great Goodfellow, Hilley, Harley, Gray and McInnes forward line that scored 100 goals in 34 games to finish third in the 1960/61 season. His last match was against Celtic on 11 May 1962, before being transferred to Newcastle United.

Alec Harley made his debut against Stenhousemuir on 10 August 1957 and he soon established himself as a centre forward, breaking the club goalscoring record in 1960/61 when he scored 42 goals. This was a record number of goals for a Thirds player whilst playing in Division One. Alec played his last game on 11 May 1962 against Celtic and was then sold to Manchester City.

Hi-Hi Highlanders Due In Seattle Sunday

Y ROLF STROMBERG

One of the most colorful d talented soccer teams Scotland's athletic history ll stir dust and stretch tting in High School Me- orial Stadium Sunday ght at 7 o'clock.

Third Lanark Football ub will match its interna- nal skills with the North- st All-Stars, drawn from Seattle, Portland d Vancouver.

Traipsing across Canada a leisurely way, the Scots ve engaged Birmingham y of the English Football League in a series of tus- sles, narrowly losing the last contest, 3-2, in Toronto.

HIGHEST scoring team ever in Scottish football. Third Lanark is managed by an almost legendary fig- ure in the Highlands, George Young, captain of the Scottish international team and a former fullback and center-half.

Big Geordie holds more Scottish international rec- ords than any other indi- vidual north of the border.

And he has molded Third Lanark in his image. Known at home as the Hi-Hi, the scarlet-and-white clad Lan- arks have captured virtually every football title extant in Scotland — including the Scottish Cup, Scottish League Championship in both divisions, Glasgow Cup and Glasgow Charity Cup.

LED BY rugged center- forward Alec Harley, who has eclipsed a 30-year scor- ing record, Third Lanark represents a side that likes to go hard after goals. In their league games this year, the club tallied more than 40.

Harley, who is the target of high-priced lures from English soccer teams, is abetted by the "Golden Cra- nium" of Matt Gray, who has headed 37 goals in the last two seasons. Fans promptly dubbed him Gold- en Cranium. Gray practices by leaping for hours at a ball suspended from the ceiling.

Then, there's 21-year-old David Hilley, the inside- right who wears a price tag of $125,000.

PAIRED WITH him is tiny Joe McInnes, deemed the best in Scotland position. Third signed him for $2 has been offered up $100,000 for his tale

On defense, the have the smallest g er in Scotland, din John Robertson, nir in the nets. He ha termed the best "u goalie" in all the Sh

All told, the All-St have their hands (busy Sunday. Howe pre-game test agair Vancouver stars las end, the Seattleites very well, winning

ALEX HARLEY
Scots' Top Scorer

MATT GRAY
He Uses His Head

DAVID HILLEY
$120,000 Price Tag

JOE McINNES
Tiny But Plenty Tricky

GEORGE YOU
Scotland's Great

Third Lanark toured the United States and Canada in May/June 1961. During the tour they met Birmingham City three times, with honours even as both teams won a match, while the other was drawn.

5 November 1960, League match at Cathkin, Third Lanark 6 Dundee United 1. A cross from Thirds' Dave Hilley finds no takers as Dundee United goalkeeper Rolando Ugolini and centre half Ron Yeats watch closely. Yeats went on to star for Liverpool in the Shankly era.

Dave Hilley turns away after scoring Thirds second goal as Dundee United defender Ron Yeats can only look on in anguish.

Players in dispute. As the 1961 official team photograph was being taken, McInnes, Gray, Hilley and Harley, who had all refused terms for the new season, were on the Pavilion balcony watching the photograph being taken below.

Third Lanark, 1961/62. From left to right, back row: Goodfellow, Ward, McGillivray, McKinlay, Cunningham, Robertson, McCormack, Smith, McCallum, Caldwell, Lewis, Tom McNiven (Trainer). Front row: George Young (Manager), Bryce, Grant, Japp, McColl, Reilly, Davis, Robb, Gallagher, McInally, Muir, McCool.

10 March 1962, Scottish Cup Quarter-final at Parkhead, Celtic 4 Third Lanark 4. Chalmers of Celtic shows his delight as his side score to fight back from 1-3 down. On the ground is Thirds 'keeper Robertson with McCormack and Gray in attendance.

Third Lanark defenders Robb, McCormack, McGillivray and 'keeper Robertson cannot prevent Celtic from scoring. Thirds were 3-1 ahead at half-time.

The old stand being demolished in June 1962. Thirds played at Hampden until the new stand was ready. The old stand had for years been the but of many jokes – if it was raining, they said, you were better out on the terracing as the stand was known to leak. In the late 1940s, when it caught fire, the crowd were asking the firemen to let it burn!

26 November 1960, League match at Shawfield, Clyde 2 Third Lanark 4. Herd and Robertson of Clyde watch as Thirds 'keeper Robertson is beaten, only for the ball to go past the post. Thirds defenders in the picture are Caldwell and Cunningham.

21 September 1963, League match at Cathkin, Third Lanark 1 Dundee 2. Gilzean of Dundee rises to beat Thirds 'keeper Mitchell and full-backs Lewis and Dickson.

8 April 1963, Glasgow Cup Final, Hampden Park, Third Lanark 2 Celtic 1. From left to right: Lewis, Spence, Robertson, McInnes, Baird, Cunningham, Davis, Goodfellow, Reilly, McGillivray and McMorran. This was the last trophy to be won by the club.

Matt Gray leaves the Cathkin field for the last time on 25 February 1963 after playing against East Fife in the Scottish Cup. The game finished 1-1. Matt made his first team debut for Thirds on 7 December 1957 against Hibernian at Easter Road. The team on that day read: Robertson, Smith, Brown, Kelly, Lewis, Slingsby, McInnes, Craig, Allan, Gray and Callan. The result was a 4-0 win for Hibs. The team in his last game read: Robertson, McGillivray, Cunningham, Reilly, Robb, Baird, McInally, Goodfellow, Benison, Gray and McInnes.

BARCLAYS BANK LIMITED
ARDWICK, MANCHESTER,
8, ARDWICK GREEN, MANCHESTER, 13.

Manchester. 6 MAY 1963

Pay the Third Lanark Athletic Club Ltd.
Thirty one thousand and one pounds — £31,001—0—0.

For and on behalf of MANCHESTER CITY FOOTBALL CLUB LIMITED

Matt was then transferred to Manchester City for a club record fee of £31,001, the one pound creating a record for a Thirds player being transferred to another club. *Above*: a copy of the cheque from Manchester City to pay for Matt Gray's fee.

MATT GRAY ON ICE AT CATHKIN 1963

The freeze-up of 1963 allows Matt Gray to put in some ice hockey practice.

Third Lanark, 1963/64. From left to right, back row: Connell, Dickson, Paul, Evans, Geddes, Cunningham. Front row: Todd, Bryce, Graham, Black, Buckley.

Third Lanark, 1963/64. From left to right, back row: Anderson, Murray, Little, Mitchell, Kerr, Paterson, McKay. Front row: McGillivray, Davis, Lewis, Brownlee, McLeod, McMorran.

20 April 1963, League match at Parkhead, Celtic 2 Third Lanark 1. Thirds 'keeper Robertson makes a save, watched by defenders Davis and McGillivray. The familiar Celtic No.10 is ex-Thirds star Bobby Craig.

This time Thirds 'keeper Robertson punches clear from Bobby Craig as defender Sammy Baird looks on.

14 March 1964, League match at Palmerston Park, Queen of the South 2 Third Lanark 4. Max Murray of Third Lanark turns away after scoring, with Queens 'keeper Ball on his knees. Also on one knee is Thirds Mike Jackson who scored a hat-trick in the match.

24 February 1965, Scottish Cup replay at East End Park, Dunfermline Athletic 2 Third Lanark 2. Thirds 'keeper Evan Williams and defenders May and McKay try to prevent Dunfermline from scoring. The tie went to a third game at Tynecastle, which Thirds lost 4-2.

Third Lanark, 1964/65. From left to right, back row: R. Evans (Manager), McGillivray, Davis, Connor, Little, McCormack, Geddes, J. Florence (Trainer). Front row: Todd, Jackson, Murray, McKay, Black.

Third Lanark, 1964/65. From left to right, back row: May, McKay, Williams, Connell, Little, Geddes, J. Florence (Trainer). Front row: Murray, Kilgannon, Baillie, Jackson, Kirk.

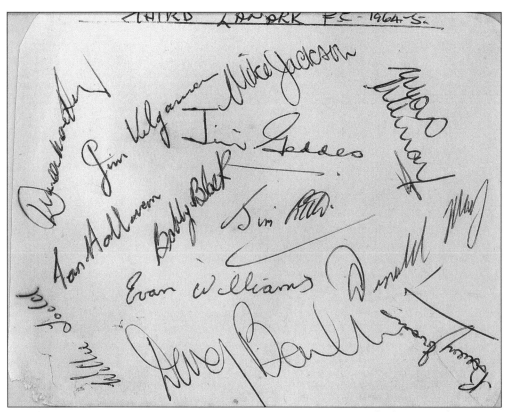

Autographs from 1964/65...

...and the last season of 1966/67.

THIRD LANARK A.C. LTD.

HI-HI NEWS

Official Programme

No. 396

No. 20	FIRST DIVISION **THIRD LANARK v. DUNFERMLINE ATH.**	SAT., 10th APRIL, 1965 Price 3d.

The last home programme ever produced.

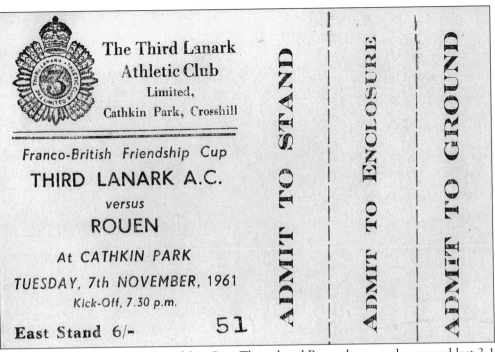

The Third Lanark
Athletic Club
Limited,
Cathkin Park, Crosshill

Franco-British Friendship Cup

THIRD LANARK A.C.

versus

ROUEN

At CATHKIN PARK

TUESDAY, 7th NOVEMBER, 1961

Kick-Off, 7.30 p.m.

East Stand 6/-   51

ADMIT TO STAND

ADMIT TO ENCLOSURE

ADMIT TO GROUND

Thirds in the Franco British Friendship Cup. They played Roeun home and away and lost 2-1 on both occasions.

THIRD LANARK ATHLETIC CLUB LIMITED.

SEASON 19 / 19

COMPLIMENTARY

ADMIT TO CAR PARK

Name...

Address..

....

ROBERT SHANKLY (Manager)

For Conditions see over

.A complimentary ticket for the car park.

Players from the 1964/65 season. David Brady was an outside left who made his debut against Hibs on 8 August 1964. He is featured on p.4 in the over-50s match of 1997.

Pat Buckley, an outside left, made his debut against Falkirk on 8 September 1962. He played his last game on 8 February 1964 before transferring to Wolves.

Willie Todd debuted for the Thirds against Dundee at the Cathkin, 10 August 1963. He played 27 games as an outside right in the 1964/65 season, when the club used 33 players in 51 games.

Jim Little was a centre half who first played for Third Lanark on 20 March 1963 and went on to play in the team's very last game, the match against Dumbarton on 28 April 1967.

More players from the 1964/65 season. The left-back Tony Connell played 123 games for the club and was in the team for the last game at Dumbarton. He went on to play for St Mirren and Queen of the South after Thirds folded.

Joe Davis, another left-back, made his debut against Inverness Caley on 17 February 1962. He played more than 80 games for the club before being transferred to Hibernian.

Stewart Mitchell was signed from Newcastle United in 1963, making his debut as Thirds' goalkeeper on 10 August. His last game for the club was against St Johnstone on 6 March 1965.

Alan McKay debuted on 19 October 1963 against Hearts. A left half, he played 97 games for the club, including the last match at the Cathkin – against Queen of the South on 25 April 1967. After the demise of Third Lanark he went on to play for Motherwell and Dumbarton.

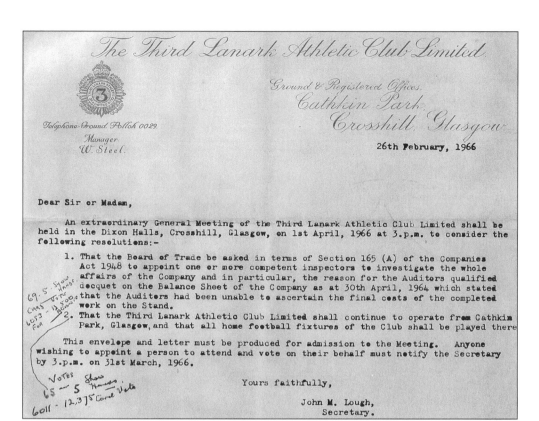

The Third Lanark Athletic Club Limited

Telephone—Ground. Pollok 0029.
Manager:
W. Steel.

Ground & Registered Offices.
Cathkin Park.
Crosshill, Glasgow.

26th February, 1966

Dear Sir or Madam,

An extraordinary General Meeting of the Third Lanark Athletic Club Limited shall be held in the Dixon Halls, Crosshill, Glasgow, on 1st April, 1966 at 3.p.m. to consider the following resolutions:-

1. That the Board of Trade be asked in terms of Section 165 (A) of the Companies Act 1948 to appoint one or more competent inspectors to investigate the whole affairs of the Company and in particular, the reason for the Auditors qualified docquet on the Balance Sheet of the Company as at 30th April, 1964 which stated that the Auditors had been unable to ascertain the final costs of the completed work on the Stand.

2. That the Third Lanark Athletic Club Limited shall continue to operate from Cathkin Park, Glasgow, and that all home football fixtures of the Club shall be played there

This envelope and letter must be produced for admission to the Meeting. Anyone wishing to appoint a person to attend and vote on their behalf must notify the Secretary by 3.p.m. on 31st March, 1966.

Yours faithfully,

John M. Lough,
Secretary.

The letter above indicates signs of trouble ahead and unfortunately this proved to be the case

The last known team photograph, Third Lanark, 1965/66. From left to right, back row: Connell, Baillie, Williams, Jackson, Little, McKay. Front row: Miller, McLaughlan, Fyfe, Kilgannon, Henderson.

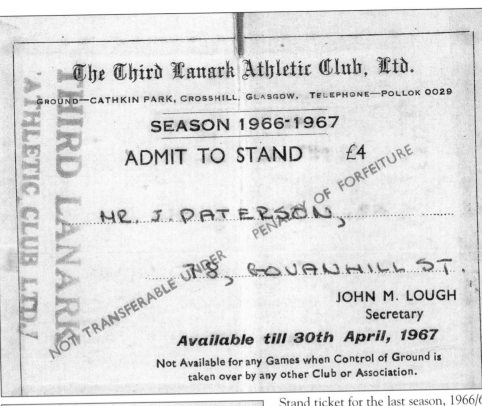

The Third Lanark Athletic Club, Ltd.

GROUND—CATHKIN PARK, CROSSHILL, GLASGOW.   TELEPHONE—POLLOK 0029

SEASON 1966-1967

ADMIT TO STAND   £4

MR. J. PATERSON,

NOT TRANSFERABLE UNDER PENALTY OF FORFEITURE

8, GOVANHILL ST.

JOHN M. LOUGH
Secretary

Available till 30th April, 1967

Not Available for any Games when Control of Ground is
taken over by any other Club or Association.

Stand ticket for the last season, 1966/67.

THE THIRD LANARK ATHLETIC CLUB,
LIMITED.

Press Messenger
Ticket

DAILY EXPRESS.

R. EVANS,
Secy./Manager.

Press messenger ticket for the last
season, 1966/67.

Hugh McLaughlan made his debut in the 1965/66 season and featured in the last home and away matches in April 1967. He scored in the home match against Queen of the South in a 3-3 draw and was at right half in the last game at Dumbarton.

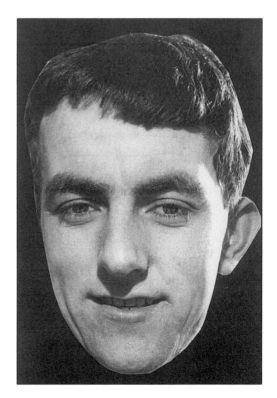

Hugh Stewart made his debut in the 1966/67 season. He played in the last home match but missed the last away match against Dumbarton.

Drew Busby only played eleven games for Thirds and they were the club's last eleven games. He scored the last goal in the club's history in a 5-1 defeat at Dumbarton on 28 April 1967.

FRIDAY, APRIL 28
SCOTTISH LEAGUE—DIV. II

Dumbarton (1) 5 (Kirk 2, Mc-Millan 2, McCormack)   500

Third Lanark (0) 1 (Busby)

Dumbarton: Crawford; Curran, Jardine; Harra, McGhee, Lynas; Moffatt, McCormack, Watson, Mc-Millan, Kirk.

Third Lanark: Russell; Connell, Heaney; McLaughlin, Little, McEwan; Rundell, Craig, Busby, May, Kinnaird.

The last line-up and ninety-five years of existence ended. The club was gone but never to be forgotten, playing their part in the formation of organised Scottish football from 1872.

Cathkin Park in June 1967. The gates are now firmly closed.

Cathkin Park in June 1967. The ground has that deserted look.

Above and below: Cathkin Park, 1968. The end of an era as the vandals have moved in.